Marc-Rian Stubbs

This book is dedicated to my grandson Marc-Rian Stubbs, a unique, quirky, intelligent young man who loved & adored cats and all creatures big & small.

Love You Always, your Nan

The Amazing Max and the Young Inventor

by Caroline Nelson

Illustrations by Paul Nash

It was a cold Winter morning. So cold all the little kitties in the animal rescue centre were cuddled up together fast asleep. All except for one small kitten who lay shivering all on his own.

This frighten little kitten had not slept a wink.
He was sad, confused, and very alone.

Just then the door opened and a cheery voice called out ...
"How are my beautiful kitties today?"

" Wakie wakie everyone ... rise and shine."

"Let's have a roll call sweet peas, let me see who is here today ... yes I see Rocco, there's Sammy, and little Alice."

"But wait a minute where is the new boy Max?"

Cute little ragdoll Alice curled in and out around Miss Vicki's legs.

In a sweet timid little voice Alice said "It was the bully boy Rocco he frightened Max, he's a naughty meanie."

Miss Vicki couldn't understand kitty talk but she could see Alice was upset.

Just then one of the bigger kittens strutted up and boxed Alice in the ear.

"Ouch that hurt Rocco!" cried Alice.

"Stop that immediately Rocco ... you are a very naughty kitty. You should never hit someone and especially a little girl" cried Miss Vicki as she bent down to pat Alice.

But Rocco just stuck his nose in the air ... and strode off with his tail sailing high ... swishing back and forth just like a fluffy duster.

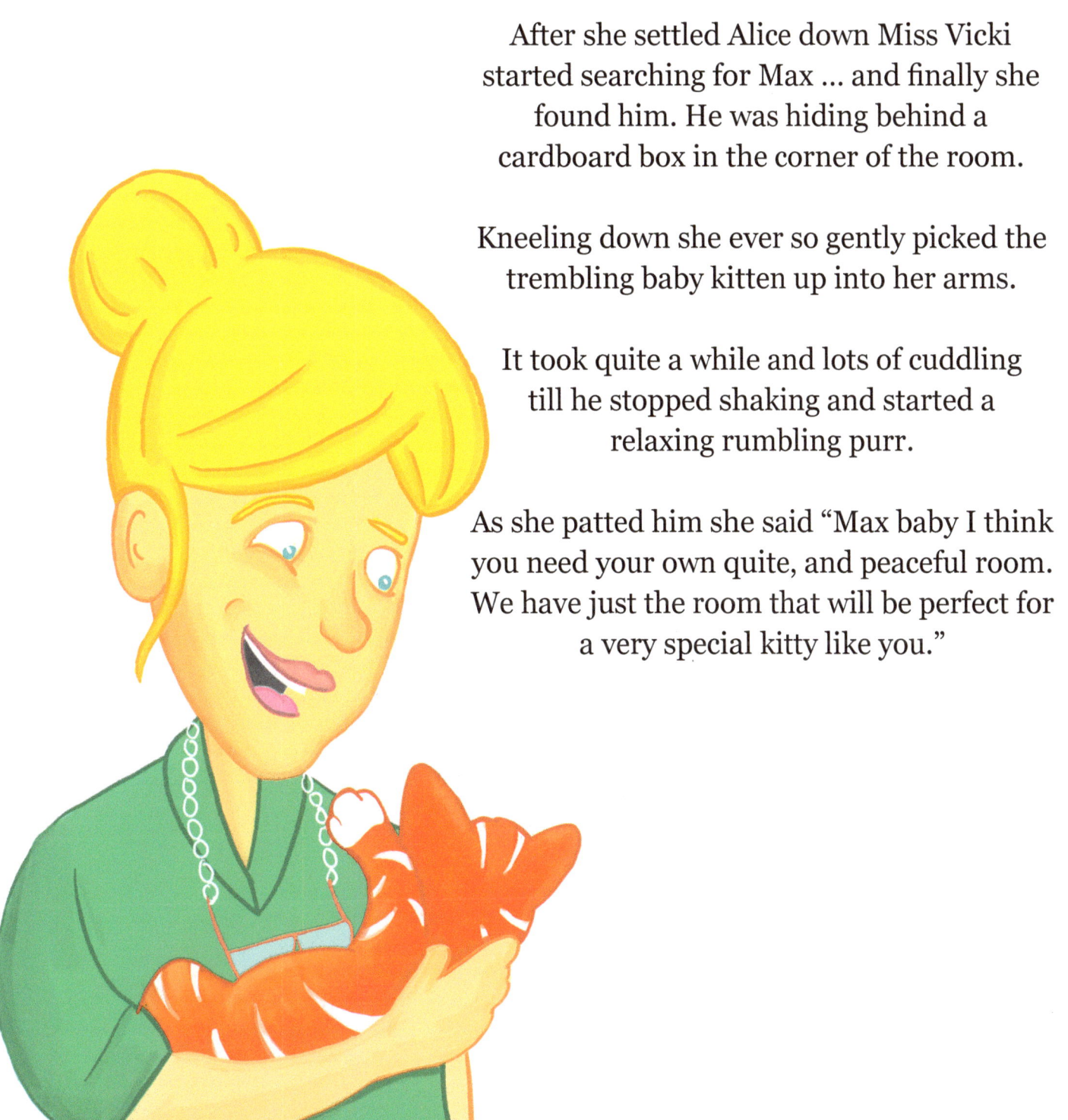

After she settled Alice down Miss Vicki started searching for Max ... and finally she found him. He was hiding behind a cardboard box in the corner of the room.

Kneeling down she ever so gently picked the trembling baby kitten up into her arms.

It took quite a while and lots of cuddling till he stopped shaking and started a relaxing rumbling purr.

As she patted him she said "Max baby I think you need your own quite, and peaceful room. We have just the room that will be perfect for a very special kitty like you."

Alice and Sammy ran to the door to say bye to Max.

While the nasty Rocco arched his back, hissed and yelled "Don't come back you're not welcome you weirdo! Ha ha you've only got three legs, and no tail … no one will ever want to adopt you!" said nasty Rocco.

After this unpleasant exit it took Miss Vicki quite some time to settle the sad kitty into his new room.

But eventually after lots of cuddles he fell asleep in her arms.

She gently placed him on the soft cushion bed and quietly closed the door.

Today was Sunday a busy day at the animal rescue and rehoming centre.

It was when many humans visited hoping to find the perfect pet.

A pet to take home and lavish with love and care. To become part of their forever family.

All the animal carers cleaned, tidied, emptied litter trays, and made everything ship shape and sparkling to impress the visitors.

While the kittens and older cats all groomed themselves … licking and fluffing their fur coats till they were shiny and soft.

Then they excitedly waited to see who would be chosen? And wondered what would their new homes be like?

While all this activity went on little Max was mostly undisturbed.

A few people walked by his "Special Needs" room but no one come in to meet or play with him ... he was very alone!

But everyone loves little kittens. Especially perfect cute ones, and even ones with "attitude".

So at the end of the day Sammy, Alice, and even "attitude" boy Rocco had all found new forever families.

Two weeks went by and several new kittens came into the centre. And just as quickly found new homes and left.

But still little Max stayed all alone in his room. Only Miss Vicki spent time playing and cuddling him ... and that was only when she had time.

Unfortunately for the little handicapped kitten no one else ventured in to meet him. Or even show any interest ... people would briefly look in and then quickly walk away.

And so time just drifted by with Max covering his eyes and snoozing away in his safe lonely room ....

The door whooshed open and Miss Vicki came in clapping her hands to wake Max up from his snoozing.

Brightly she chuckled "Today is the day Maxie I feel it's going to be your lucky day. Let's get you all spruced up in your Sunday best fur coat."

Max loved Miss Vicki but he wasn't optimistic.

He just knew today would be like all the other days.

Because no one wanted a damaged little kitten like him.

Like all Sunday's he could hear lots of activity happening. Kittens being chosen, saying their good byes to each other.

This made Max a little sad … so many others were leaving on a grand adventure …. but not him….

So he curled up on his cushion closed his eyes and drifted off to sleep.

But what was that? The door was being opened …

Sleepy Max opened one eye to see who was there.

Would it be Miss Vicki bringing him a little treat? But no … it wasn't her … it was a large man and a pretty lady.

Who are they? And what did they want? He tightly shut his eyes, held his breath, and waited.

They came into the room.

The lady bent to stroke his fur, ever so very gently.

Then the man picked Max up and had a good look at his little body and said "Vicki told us you're a special little man, and we can see you are."

Gently tickling Max under his chin he went on to say "Max we have a big home with a sunny backyard would you like to come live with us?"

The special little man looked up and purred a happy tune, which in cat talk said "Yes please."

And that's how Max the three legged, no tail kitten found a family to love and care for him.

But the story doesn't end there. Oh no there's much more to this tale.

Kate and Bill were the perfect family for a special needs pet.

Nothing was ever too much trouble as long as their adored kitty or "fur-baby" as Kate called him was happy.

And Max's sweet nature returned all the love and affection right back to Kate and Bill.

Life was good. But there was one small problem.

Bill was a doctor and Kate a nurse and they worked long hours at their jobs.

This left Max alone much of the time, which wasn't too bad.

Especially as Kate would leave the television on all day to keep him company.

This kept Max entertained and it also allowed his imagination to run riot.

Such possibilities opened up to him … he could run … he could fly … he could be a Super Hero!

But mostly in his imagination and dreams he could see himself running on all four legs.

Oh to have four legs like other cats … and a tail too!

After a while Max learned to hop and scoot around on his three legs.

And one day he eventually managed to get through the cat door that Bill had made for him.

He bravely ventured out into the wonderful unknown of his sunny backyard.

It was in the backyard where he met his new best friend Seymour.

Seymour was a blue tongue lizard.

Max thought Seymour was old and wise just like Yoda the Jedi Master in the Star Wars films he watched on TV.

Max didn't even notice Seymour at first. He was too busy checking out all the cool things to see, smell and play with.

So you can imagine his shock when he heard a deep voice say "Hey kid watch it … you nearly knocked me off my perch, I'm sunbathing."

"Sorry" said Max "I didn't see you."

"But who are you? And what are you? And why are you in my backyard?"

"My name is Seymour and I'm a blue tongue lizard. And hang on a minute this is not only your backyard … there are lots of others who live here."

"And I've lived in this hollow log for many years. So what do you think of that young fellow?"

Max was very excited and spoke so fast his words all jumbled together "My name's Max and I think it's cool living in a log and will you be my friend?" he said all in one breath.

And that's how Max and Seymour met and became the very best of friends.

Max found Seymour understanding and kind, and never once did he make fun of Max's lack of tail or missing leg.

Or his dream of one day being able to run around like other cats.

Each day they would meet in a sunny spot in the back yard to chat.

Seymour had many wonderful adventurous stories to share.

One day Max found Seymour standing next to the fence.

"I won't be around for the next couple of days kid …. I'm off to visit my friend Bugzy" he said.

"Who's Bugzy" said Max.

"Bugzy is my oldest friend, and she's the tabby cat who lives next door" said Seymour.

"But … but why are you visiting her?" a slightly upset Max asked. He was going to miss his friend.

Seymour chuckled "Have you heard the unusual sounds coming from Bugzy's house? They seemed to go on for ages."

"In any case I like to know what's happening in my neighbourhood."

"I think the young inventor could be up to something … and I'm thinking it might be time for me to investigate. See you later!"

And with this quick goodbye and before Max could even ask "Who or what is a young inventor?" Seymour had pushed his way through a tiny hole at the bottom of the fence and disappeared.

Max just stood there with his mouth gapping open in amazement.

He couldn't wait till Seymour came back.

There were so many questions he needed to ask.

So for two long days Max kept a look out to see if Seymour was back.

On the third morning he went out to the hole in the fence and just as he bent down to look, out popped Seymour.

"Hi kid how's it going?" said his best mate.

"Great … but I can't wait to hear all about your visit with Bugzy and the young inventor" said a very excited Max.

"Well, have I've got lots to tell you" said Seymour with a twinkle in his eyes.

"And guess what?" the wise old lizard chuckled. "I might even be able to fix you up with a new tail and fourth leg."

"So what do you think about that, young fella?"

Once again Max stood with his mouth open in amazement.

"What do you mean" Max stuttered "a new tail and a leg … is that possible?"

"It is when you live next door to a truly talented young inventor it seems" laugh Seymour.

Over the next hours Seymour told Max all about his exciting news.

It seemed that Bugzy and his friend Marc the young inventor had a very special dream connection.

This amazingly allowed them to share their thoughts while they were sleeping.

So during their dream time Marc the young inventor learnt about an amazing kitten called Max.

A special kitten who had no tail and only three legs … a kitten who dreamed of being like other kittens and cats.

On waking twelve year old Marc was very excited.
He'd dreamed of an amazing invention he could make.

One he could enter into the 3D Printing Challenge competition this school holidays.

He would make the disabled kitty next door a new tail and leg… how cool would that be!

Marc raced next door to speak with his neighbours Kate and Bill.

He excitedly explained about the competition and how he hoped they would agree to let him create a new tail and leg for their beloved Max.

"Whoo Hoo" thought Max jumping up onto Marc's lap and purring his plea own tail and fourth leg, I'm so happy". The humans didn't know what Max was saying but they could see he was very pleased.

And so began a new chapter in the tale of The Amazing Max.

After several days of measurements, trial and error, and much whirring of the 3D printer ... finally the time had come for Max to be fitted with his new tail and leg.

Marc's mother helped by covering the 3D printed plastic with fake fur to match Max's fur coat.

Everyone gathered around and once the last buckle had been fastened ... whoosh Max took off around the room like a whirlwind.

"Wow just watch him go" said everyone at once, clapping and laughing.

Max raced out the sliding door and into the backyard. "Seymour! Seymour come and see!"

He raced around showing Seymour how fast he could go, and thanked his friend over and over again for helping to make his dream come true.

The next morning he was up bright and early to go with the young inventor to the judging of the 3D Printing Challenge.

There were many very interesting entries but none quite like Marc's. Because who could top an excited kitty scooting around and around the room to the gleeful audience yelling "Watch that kitten go!"

The judging took some time but finally the winner was announced.

"And the winner is Marc Stubbs with his entry of a device to help disabled cats" said Mr Smith the judge.

"And we would also like to say a special thank you to Max ... you are the inspiration for this winning entry."

Marc and Max became overnight celebrities with photos and stories written in the local newspaper … and interviews on television.

Everyone wanted to meet The Amazing Max and Marc the Young Inventor.

Then one day Bill came home from working in the hospital's children ward with some wonderful news to share.

"Guess what? My boss asked me if Max and Marc could come visit the sick children, to help cheer them up" he said.

And Kate laughingly said "And guess what? My boss asked if they could visit the residents at the retirement home too.

Life had suddenly become very exciting … wonderful things can happen and they had for a sweet little kitty … and a special caring young inventor.

So that is the tale of a boy with a gift of creating ... and how he helped a special kitty who dreamed of having four legs ... and a tail of course.

And how they became the "Super Duo" hero's' of sick little children and elderly people ... and Max the little kitten was never lonely ever again.

The End

www.ingramcontent.com/pod-product-compliance
Lightning Source LLC
Chambersburg PA
CBHW061816290426
44110CB00026B/2887